RECLAIMING THE VILLAGE

PARENTS TAKING BACK THEIR RIGHTFUL PLACE IN THE FAMILY

Kathy Starks

ISBN: 978-1-948985-09-3

...Your children are not your children.

They are the sons and daughters of Life's longing for itself.

They come through you but not from you,

And though they are with you they belong not to you.

You may give them your love but not your thoughts,

For they have their own thoughts.

You may house their bodies but not their souls,

For their souls, dwell in the house of tomorrow,

which you cannot visit, not even in your dreams.

You may strive to be like them, but seek not to make them like you.

For life goes not backward nor tarries with yesterday.

You are the bows from which your children as living arrows are sent forth.

The archer sees the mark upon the path of the infinite, and He bends

You with His might His arrows may go swift and far.

Let your bending in the archer's hand be for gladness;

For even as He loves the arrows that flies, so

He loves also the bow that is stable.

- Kahlil Gibran, from The Prophet

REVIEWS

"If you are a parent or someone who plays a parenting role in a child's life, you need to read this book. Reclaiming the Village gives you the blueprint for regaining or strengthening the foundation in your family. Kathy has taken her many years of experience and written a gritty, heart-filled, and knowledge-based prescription for making the family better. This will be your first step in creating a family positioned to manage in today's world."

~ Deborah Johnson AKA, "DJ" the Dream Coach President, Goal Minded, LLC "What's Your Game Plan?"

"Kathy provides parents and caregivers with tons of practical advice in a very readable, user-friendly manner. I highly recommend this read for all parents as a guidebook on one of life's most important adventures."

~ Joan Zeller LMSW, ATR

DEDICATION

In loving memory of my parents, who by their examples showed me the value of the village.

CONTENTS

PREFACE

As a school counselor for almost thirty years, I have had the pleasure and the privilege to be involved in the lives of hundreds of children, primarily middle school children. Although I have not raised any children of my own, I have had the unique perspective of having a window into the souls of countless teens and their families.

Over the years I have seen all types of families--some good, some not so good, and everything in between. This is not an indictment on all families, but simply a commentary on some of the families and situations I have encountered. Most families are doing all the right things and still their children can struggle with unforeseen situations. The families that seem to work well have a sense of unconditional love and support of their children regardless of family circumstances. I have felt honored and humbled that families and kids have put their faith and trust in me to help them navigate the murky waters of middle school. I spent my entire career as a middle school counselor. Since retirement, I have been blessed to work part-time in one of the high schools in my district. It has been an eye-opening experience to see so many of my middle schoolers as high school students now and to have an opportunity to see some of the challenges they face.

In *Reclaiming the Village*, I have attempted to share stories of what works and what doesn't work when dealing with teens, and the lessons I've learned about middle school and now high school children. What lies ahead in this book is meant to be an anecdotal account of my interactions and relationships with numerous students and their families. While I have cited the work of others in some chapters in the area of teen development, this book is not intended to be research-based in nature. I hope that in reading this book you find humor, some good information, and inspiration as you journey through these sometimes-difficult teen years with your children. *Reclaiming the Village* attempts to examine some of the difficulties teens are having today and ways that the family can better support children so they can go out into the world with confidence, ready to face the challenges of adulthood.

INTRODUCTION:
THE VILLAGE

What has happened to the Village? Does it exist today? At a time in our lives, when there is plenty of access and opportunities abound, why are so many young people struggling with issues of anxiety, depression, and suicide? These were some of the questions I had when I started working with the high school students several years ago. I recently asked my 20-year-old Godson, Camron his thoughts about why teens have so much anxiety and depression. He summed it up in one word: competition. He said that everything is very competitive now. From getting good grades to getting into stellar universities to excelling in sports. For many students, their self-worth is dictated by how "successful" they appear. But what is success, and by whose account? Is success for the young person based on what their friends say is success, or their parents, or both? That answer may be different depending on the student. Camron believes that competition is what is causing many students and some of his peers to be stressed and anxious.

High school students today are smarter than ever. Many are taking advanced placement courses, starting their own businesses, and working. With all that young people have accomplished there are still many who struggle with anxiety and depression. What are the causes? Jummy Olawale, Licensed Professional Clinical Counselor believes that stress among teens and young adults comes from having too many choices. In her clinical counseling practice, Jummy sees many students struggling because they can't narrow down the plethora of choices for course selections or areas of study they may want to focus on. When she worked as an on-campus counselor at The Ohio State University, Jummy received the highest number of counseling requests from freshman who were stressed out about coursework and choices.

There is an old African proverb that states it takes a village to raise a child. That statement has never been truer. With Generation Z's text messaging and videogaming, children have lost their connection with the village. Youth today are used to instant gratification, and when they can't have that they often don't know how to cope.

Years ago, the neighborhood, and extended family were part of the village. The village seems to have disappeared. Extended family is spread across the country, and most people do not know their neighbors. In the past, if you got in trouble in the neighborhood, you also got in trouble at home. Not so true now. Today, if a parent contacts another parent about a child's behavior, that could turn into an argument. Some parents don't want to communicate with each other anymore.

Recent studies have indicated that childhood obesity is reaching alarming rates. Kids are spending anywhere from three to five hours a day watching television or playing video games. Youth are not getting outside to play anymore. This fact is has led to an increasing number of young people who don't know how to communicate, settle disputes, or interact appropriately. Parents are overwhelmed dealing with work, finances, and household matters, and it is much easier to let kids play video games and watch television. If children feel that they cannot connect with their parents, they often turn to risky activities. In his book *The Second Family*, Ron Taffel states that children join gangs when they don't feel they have the love and support of their "first family."[1] When asked about the increase in anxiety and depression in young people. Dr. Keith Bell of the Ohio State University believes "that young people, especially college students, run from adversity." He also believes that young people lack the vision to see future possibilities. The very idea or notion of family has changed so much over the last few decades, and today that idea of the family still exists along with a myriad of other types of family units.

The advent of great technological influences in our lives has had an important impact on families. Kids are in internet chat rooms, meeting strangers online, and playing inappropriate games. Parents are often oblivious to this fact. Jummy Olawale believes that the village is especially lost for the adults. In previous generations, parents were able to lean on and receive advice and support from their parents or other elders in the community. Many grandparents and other family members are not around for younger parents. She also believes that parents are experiencing "pressured parenting." They feel pressure to be all and do all for their children, be at every event, plan every activity, and still attempt to work and have a life of their own. And when you add privilege and affluence, the pressures are even greater.

When I was growing up in the sixties and seventies, we played board games as a family or watched movies together. Many kids now are held up in their bedrooms or basement with little to no interaction with their parents during the evening. Often, parents comment that their children do not talk to them and rarely tell them how they are feeling or share issues about which they are concerned. Parents often feel disconnected from their children and lack the skills or abilities to reconnect. Some children feel that their parents don't understand them or seemingly don't care to understand them, so the children shut down. If children feel that they cannot connect with their parents, they often turn to risky behaviors.

How can families learn how to connect with each other, and get back on track? I believe honest open communication is the way to keep families together. In the following pages, I will share stories of kids and families that persevered, made it through the tough middle school years, and soared in high school and beyond.

I was blessed to grow up in a neighborhood with only two streets. All the families knew each other and that was my "village." The other interesting and unique quality about my neighborhood was that it was an African American middle-class neighborhood within a predominately white middle class suburb. I also attended a predominately white high school in spite of the fact that my neighborhood was African American. This gave me a unique opportunity to have an outstanding education but be immersed in my culture at home. My neighbors were professional individuals that allowed me to see and believe that I could achieve and have access to those same experiences. The neighbors taught me the value of hard work, setting goals, and supporting each other. Those neighbors taught me the value of the village.

There are so many things causing the breakdown of families today. Drugs and alcohol, anxiety, and depression, absent parents, and busy schedules. How do we get back to creating the families of the past and reclaim the village?

The diagram below is the beginning of how we reclaim the village. Parents, teachers, and community members need to work together to ensure the success of young people today. We are all in this together, and together we can make a difference in the lives of children.

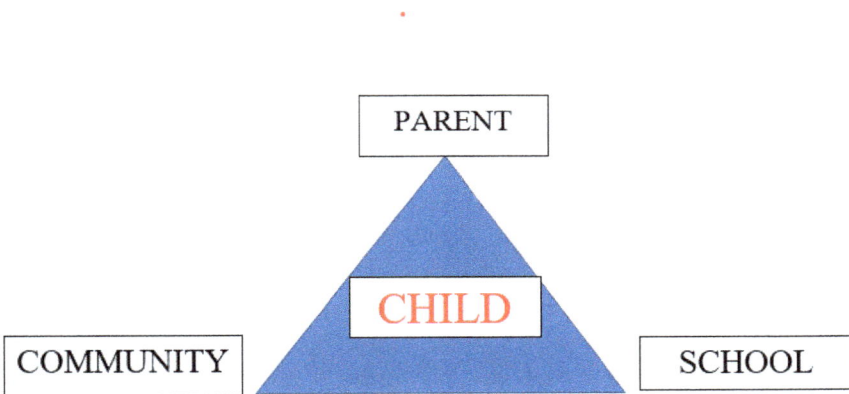

PARENT

CHILD

COMMUNITY

SCHOOL

ENABLING BEHAVIORS

We cripple people who are capable of walking because we choose to carry them. ~ Christie Williams

In reading the Kahlil Gibran passage regarding children, "Your children are not your children...they come through you but not from you..." that stuck with me the first time I heard it. I was first made aware of this passage as part of my career development training with the Worthington School District. Mary Lynne Musgrove, a longtime career counselor in Worthington, worked with many teachers and counselors in the area of career development. She would often share this passage as she worked with teachers. Most parents love and cherish their children so fiercely that they do not realize the need to teach their child confidence and independence at the earliest of ages.

There is no doubt if you ask any parent what their hopes and dreams are for their children; they would say they want their children to grow up healthy and happy and create a life of meaning and purpose for themselves. In many parents' attempts to do this they overcompensate and want to keep their children from every hurt harm and danger. Parents should indeed try to keep their children safe from physical dangers, but what about everyday difficulties that every human must overcome to achieve and be successful?

Part of this reason is fear. At an early age, parents protect their infants from the physical environment around them. They are careful not to let their children touch a hot stove or run into the street. As children grow, they gain confidence by managing the world around them. But then fear enters the parent's mind and heart. As children enter middle school and high school, parents want so desperately for their child to be successful they resort to "helping" them with their homework or asking teachers to change a grade. These behaviors are pushing children toward failure; the very thing you are trying to avoid.

A friend of mine recently asked me just how to go about teaching independence to her teenage daughter. Her question was how much should I let her do on her own? My analogy was simple. As infants are learning to crawl and then walk, they experience falls and tumbles. Parents allow these early attempts of their children to navigate the world around them. What would happen if a parent picked up their child after a nasty fall and carried them around for the next several years? The parents would end up with a handicapped child. Dr. Kirsten Smith, Director of Gifted Education for Columbus City Schools believes that parents need to give their children opportunities to experience and practice independence. When parents don't do this, they handicap their children.

Jummy Olawale agrees with this. She believes that children have little practice with difficult things because parents are acting as "shock absorbers" for their children. Children need to develop self-efficacy. Olawale says that parents can control the experiences and practice difficult things in a safe environment.

During adolescence, some parents want to fix every misstep and solve all problems. It is true that there are degrees to every choice. You certainly would not allow your child to be involved in activities that are dangerous. But parents do need to let adolescents learn to talk to their teachers about a grade dispute or settle conflicts with friends. If the child is having issues resolving the conflicts, then the parents could intervene. When I asked high school principal, Pete Scully, why he thought we have more children with anxiety and depression he stated that it's fear. Parents have a fear of failure for their children; that their children won't succeed. Parents are worried about their child's grades, whether they will be accepted into a reputable college or university, can their child navigate friendships and relationships, and on and on and on.

Fear has parents doing some crazy things like their child's homework, bailing their child out of tough situations, making excuses for uncompleted work, etc. In some cases, parents feel that if their child doesn't succeed (whatever that really is), that this is a reflection on their parenting and that they have somehow failed as a parent. Is the fear that parents are feeling related to their child's failure or their own? Some parents are so consumed and involved in their children's lives that they have lost sight of their own.

Jeff Maddox, Human Resource Director for Worthington City Schools, believes that *time* is a factor in parents minds. He explained like this: The pace of life is so fast. Parents must weigh having a "teachable moment" with their child or taking care of the problem themselves. Parents are worried that they may not have enough time to get everything done.

My longtime coworker, Lori, and I used to facilitate parent workshops throughout the school district that we work in. I would always say to parents, "Do you want to pay me now or pay me later? Are you the parent that goes to the store at 10:00 p.m. to get materials for your child so they can finish their project at midnight? Are you the parent that leaves work in the middle of the day to drop off a missing assignment to your child?" Sometimes these things are ok to do, but is this something that is standard routine for you?

Lori would always share the story of one of the basketball players she used to coach. She had a strict rule that if you forgot your basketball shoes, you could not play in the game that day. This players' parents didn't like that at all. The player was going to borrow shoes from a teammate, but Lori was clear that he would not play. That was a hard lesson for that young man to learn, but as a result, he never forgot his shoes again.

A missing assignment in middle school--while disappointing--is not the end of the world. But if a child has not learned to organize assignments and projects at an early age, what happens to that student when they go off to college? If the adults in a child's world enable them too much, they may begin to believe that they can't be successful on their own, and as a result, self-confidence erodes. In her book *The Gift of Failure*, Jessica Lahey states:

"Every time we rescue, hover, or otherwise save our children from any challenge, we send a very clear message: That we believe they are incompetent, incapable, and unworthy of our trust. Further, we teach them to be dependent on us and thereby deny them the very education in competence we are put on this earth to hand down."[1]

Deb Johnson, AKA D.J. the Sports Mom, says, "Parents believe they are helping their children, but kids feel stupid when parents do everything for them."

In speaking with Andrew Smith, an elementary principal, he made the point that parents need to let their children experience "productive struggle." They need to have struggle with a purpose. Andrew states that children need to experience struggle but also learn how to "get back up again." Andrew's wife, Dr. Kirsten Smith agrees with this statement. She believes that children can also learn from seeing their parents' struggle as well. When Kirsten defended her dissertation, she had her high school daughter there to observe the process to see what she experienced. Kirsten's daughter saw her mother working diligently over the years to complete her Ph.D. and she also saw the reward when her mother graduated. Parents have the prime opportunity to help their children when they are struggling and learn valuable lessons in the process, that will make it easier for them the next time a tough situation arises. When parents fix or solve negative situations for their children, they rob them of the productive struggle. Kids need to experience failures in life so they can learn to overcome them and make better choices in the future.

In her book, *How to Raise an Adult,* Julie Lythcott-Haims writes:

"…They don't learn to make choices or to construct possibility from the vacuum of boredom. They don't learn responsibility or accountability for their own behaviors. They don't get the chance to stumble or build resilience. They feel supremely accomplished for things they really haven't achieved on their own or, in alternative, believe they are incapable of accomplishing without us. Hell-bent on removing all risks of life and on catapulting them into college with the right brand name, we've robbed our kids of the chance to construct and know their own selves. You might say we've mortgaged their childhood in exchange for the future we imagine for them—a debt that can never be repaid."[2]

I am reminded of a young middle school boy that I worked with named Ben. Ben and I had a good relationship. He had come in and talked to me about things regarding his schedule and other things. Ben was smart and well-liked. On this day, his overinvolved mother called, asking me to change Ben's schedule. Ben was not happy with one of his elective classes. The change was easy enough to make, but I wanted to talk to Ben first. I told him that I was surprised that he didn't come in and talk to me himself. He didn't have much of a response. I told him in a very stern matter that he needed to stop having his mommy solve all his problems! I regretted that statement as soon as I said it. Ben looked at me with surprise and disbelief, but from that day on our relationship was even stronger and his mother never called me again.

I saw Ben a few years later and he gave me a big hug. He was thriving in high school. He was very involved and had many friends.

I recall another incident during the year I coached middle school volleyball (yes that was short-lived). I specifically told the parents that if their daughters had concerns about their playing time, that the girls should talk to me first. I would not entertain any parent phone calls unless the child spoke to me first. I told the parents that middle school is the time when students need to work on their problem - solving skills in an appropriate manner. I did receive one parent phone call during the season. The student did not talk to me first. Her mom told me that her daughter was uncomfortable talking to me. I did speak the student and there were no issues during the remainder of the season.

As we have seen recently in the news, wealthy parents paid

exorbitant amounts of money to make sure their children were admitted to prestigious ivy league schools. This scheme also involved bribing college athletic coaches to recruit students regardless of their athletic ability and bribing entrance exam administrators to falsify ACT and SAT answers. Felicity Huffman and Lori Loughlin were charged as part of the scheme.[3]

And it appears to me that the more privilege a parent has, the easier it is to control the narrative and enable situations for their children. Individuals with money and influence can bail their children out of situations that the average parent would not have the means to do.

In her book *The Price of Privilege*, Madeline Levine writes:

"Raising children has come to look more like a business endeavor and less like an endeavor of the heart. We are overly concerned with the 'bottom line' with how our children 'do' rather than with who are children 'are.' We pour time and attention and money into ensuring their performance, consistently making it to their soccer game while inconsistently making it the dinner table."[4]

The role of parenting is to give your children the tools to navigate the world around them so that when they leave you, they are healthy, happy, and confident, the very thing you want for them.

In other parent situations I encountered, however, parents were more than willing to give their children the tools they needed to be successful. There was one such case of a young girl I worked with at the middle school. Katie had learning disabilities. She struggled academically and socially. She was a sweet girl but did not fit in socially with her peers. Her parents were supportive and realistic about their daughter's challenges. But instead of hovering and being overprotective, they let Katie experience all the things the other students experienced. Katie blossomed in middle school and was successful in high school. She stopped by the middle school one day to visit and announced that she had gotten her driver's license! I was happy for her but surprised that she could do that, given some of her learning disabilities in middle school. Her parents had given her the confidence to try everything and were supportive of her along the way.

I recall another situation in which a mother came in desperate to speak with me. She was concerned that her daughter, Sarah was not getting ready for school in a timely manner every day and was causing her to be late for work as she would drive her daughter to school. This mother seemed very anxious and not sure what to do. This student didn't live far enough away to ride the bus, so her mom was driving her to school. This mother was enabling her daughter's behavior and didn't know what to do. I suggested that we call her daughter down to my office and have a conversation with her. When the girl arrived at my office she said to her mother, "What are you doing here?" in a very nasty tone. I was shocked and sternly let this child know that she would not speak to her mother like that in front of me. This mother seemed so intimidated by her daughter. I couldn't believe it. I tried to get this student to tell me why she couldn't ready in the morning for school without making her mother late for work. The girl just shrugged and had no real answer. So, I suggested to this mother that she let Sarah know exactly what time she planned on walking out the door. If Sarah wasn't ready to leave when her mother was, then she could walk to school. They both looked at me in disbelief. I told Sarah that the natural consequence of not being ready when her mother was ready to leave, meant that she would walk to school.

I finally was able to convince Sarah's mom to try this and Sarah reluctantly agreed. Sarah ended up walking to school once or twice, but after that was ready when her mother was ready to leave.

Some parents seem to be afraid to let their children suffer the natural consequences of their behavior. Rescuing children at every turn will only cause them to have deficits in problem-solving in the future. Jessica Lahey states, "All this swooping in and fixing make for emotionally, intellectually, and socially handicapped children, unsure of their direction or purpose without an adult on hand to guide them."[5]

As children enter early adulthood, parents envision their children forging and embarking on their own path. The question is how can young adults do that if every precept and expectation of adulthood has been done for them for the past seventeen years? One of my closest friend's sons remarked (after being in college locally for one year), "I better figure out how to do my laundry if I plan to go away to college next year." Even he realizes that so many things have been done for him.

In recent years, I've seen the trend of students going away to college, only to return home after the first semester. Parents have commented that their child couldn't handle being away from home, so they picked their children up from school as soon as the first semester finals were over. The comment is *My child can stay at home and go to school locally*. There is certainly nothing wrong with a student attending a local college or university, but the lost opportunity of being away and figuring things out on your own is missed. Even the students who do go to school locally should consider living on campus and not at home. One of my childhood friends lamented recently that she wished she would have had the opportunity to live on campus during college, because she missed out on so many of the opportunities to meet people and be involved in campus activities, and in essence, grow as a person.

I've heard other parents share stories of their children crying on the phone begging to be picked up and brought home. In some of those cases, the parents held firm and wouldn't pick up their children. As a result, those kids pushed through their anxiety about being away from home and are thriving now.

Research regarding the teenage brain indicates that by high school, teens can make better decisions and chart their territory. If teens are not allowed to do that when the consequences aren't as great, they will have much more difficulty in the future. I am reminded of a young man recently who came into the office wanting to talk about his future. He was bleary-eyed and sleepy. He went on to say that he had been up most of the night fighting with his mother. This young man was planning to work after graduation instead of starting college right away. His mother blew up and the argument ensued. He told his mom that he already had a job lined up in construction and was interested in trying this for a while. He explained to his mom that he had no idea what he would do for a major, so it didn't make sense for him to waste money going to school. When the argument continued, Brent left the house and spent the night at his girlfriend's home. His mom had been texting him all day and I told Brent that he needed to text his mom back so she would know that he was ok.

The next day, Brent came back and told me that he and his mom talked and were able to work things out. I know that some parents will freak out if their child says they are not ready to go to college right away, but forcing them to go will never end well, especially if the child has no idea what they want to do. Parents need to hear their children's point of view and come up with good strategies together. If the children have well thought out plans about what they will do if they don't go to college right away, then they are on their way to navigating early adulthood in a good way. Whether we want to believe it or not, teens want to have a sense of autonomy and control. Students who feel they have this, tend to be happier and self-motivated.

What's next:

1. Let your child do things you know they can do for themselves.
2. Don't hover.
3. Let your children experience natural consequences for poor behavior.
4. *Don't hover!*
5. Listen, as much as possible and be supportive.

MIDDLE SCHOOL AND THE TEENAGE BRAIN

The teenage zone: the stage when an adolescent's brain synapses quit firing while the rest of the body races toward adulthood. ~ Becky Freeman

"Ms. Starks, please help! My child has lost his mind! He has been doing the stupidest things lately. He's talking back to me, not doing his homework, and quite frankly, acting like someone I don't recognize anymore! What should I do! Please help!"

As a middle school counselor, I have encountered the above scenario on more than a few occasions over the years. It seems that during the middle years some students "lose" their minds, or maybe they never found it to begin with. With many pre-teens, there appears to be a time when they lose the ability to make wise and rational decisions and often get involved with risk-taking behaviors. Many times, this behavior starts to happen in the middle school years. Research indicates that the prefrontal cortex (PFC) of the brain is still developing in teens and this development could continue as late as twenty-five years of age. The prefrontal cortex is responsible for decision making and rational thought. It makes sense that teens make poor decisions during this time. In his book, *Why Do They Act That Way?* Dr. David Walsh states:

Because the prefrontal cortex's wiring is still incomplete, the adolescent PFC can't always distinguish between a good decision and a bad one, no matter how intelligent the kid is. The ongoing wiring of the PFC helps explain why smart kids do dumb things and are quick to express anger...."[1]

Research has also discovered that there are periods of blossoming and pruning during this critical period. A variety of connections are taking place in the brain. Dendrites form connections that will continue through the teen years. Some kids who have difficulty during this time end up being involved in serious risk-taking behaviors like drugs and alcohol and other dangerous activities.

Parents are often overwhelmed during the middle school years because their children's emotions are all over the place. Parents want to give their kids more freedom but are unsure exactly what to do. Parents would say to me, "I really want to chaperone the school dance, but my son/daughter told me that I am not allowed to show my face at school. What should I do?" I would tell parents that they are still the parent, and they need to be more hands on than hands off. I would tell them to come to the dance but don't "hover" around your child.

The other concern that parents have during middle school is the fact that their child is making new friends they don't know anything about. Gone are the comforts of being an elementary school room mother and knowing all the families and children. In middle school, kids are coming together with kids from several elementary schools, and they are forming new relationships. Parents are not sure whether their kids should hang out with some of the new friends they have made. I would always tell parents to invite those new friends to your house so you can meet these new friends and find out a little more about them. Are they polite? Are they interacting with your child in a positive way?

As part of my role as a middle school counselor, I facilitated classroom guidance lessons. During these lessons, we would talk about how middle school students are changing socially, emotionally, physically, and academically. I would facilitate conversations with the kids about the various changes in all these categories. Sometimes the kids would comment that they often are upset, and they don't know why, or they would do something risky and regret it later. The students would also comment that they did well in elementary school and now they are having difficulty keeping track of assignments and school projects. I would explain that during puberty, they are going through the most drastic changes that they will face in their lifetime. They are trying to manage academics, social norms, physical changes in their bodies, and sometimes emotional upheaval. It's any wonder that these kids can keep anything straight. Parents are expecting their adolescent children to be more responsible and begin taking more ownership of themselves. Teachers are expecting kids to be more responsible as a student and get things done in a timely matter or ask for help if they don't understand something. In her book *The Gift of Failure,* Jessica Lahey states:

"Middle school teachers ask students to succeed at tasks that their half-cooked, adolescent brains are not able to master, and therefore, failure is not an if proposition, it's a matter of when."[2]

As a middle school counselor, I often wondered if I could keep anything straight after helping the students navigate all the issues that arise. Parents would meet with me at the beginning of the year with fear and trepidation on their faces. Their comments were "I'm not ready for this transition," or "I am afraid my child won't make it." I remember one parent in particular whose son was on the autism spectrum. He had finished a great elementary experience, and his mother was terrified about her son coming to the middle school. She tearfully said, most of these kids don't know my son. What if he's in classes where he doesn't know anyone? Are kids going to tease him? How can I check to make sure he is getting all his work done? I tried my best to ease her fears. As the year progressed, this young man became more confident in his abilities, was able to manage the academics, and made some new friends. At the end of the year, his mother was pleasantly surprised by her sons' progress. She sheepishly recalled how distressed she was at the thought of her son's transition to middle school. She said, "You told me things would work out, and you were right. I was just so worried."

One of the topics that would always come up is the experimentation with drugs and alcohol. The adage of "Just say no!" does not work for this generation of young people. So many times, the students would say that they don't feel peer pressure to fit in by smoking or drinking. No one is calling them names or teasing them for not wanting to experiment with these things. It was more of an attitude that some kids wanted to try things just to say that they had, not that they felt pressure to. Other kids of course want to fit in or feel popular. I found that in my conversations with these kids, that the students who still told their parents everything and had a good relationship with their parents, were less likely to be involved in this type of activity. The students who were also involved in school activities or sports were also less likely to experiment with drugs and alcohol. Many studies have been conducted about the effect of drugs and alcohol on the brain. The impact on the teenage brain is more dramatic. Since the teenage brain is still developing, drug and alcohol use can impede the development of the brain. In another part of his book *Why Do They Act That Way?* Dr. Walsh states:

"Adolescents who drink a lot of alcohol end up having more memory and learning impairment than adults who drink the same amount."[3]

About twenty years ago I had a group of students who were excited about setting small fires. They participated in this activity for some time, just waiting for the thrill of seeing the flames. They couldn't explain their behavior and seemed oblivious to the possible dangers of this activity.

More recently I had another group of students engaging in a game called the "Eraser Challenge." About twenty boys were using erasers to burn their skin to see which person could erase their skin the longest, before giving into the pain. As you read this, you may be thinking, "How stupid can this be?" Most adults would agree with you. When confronted with why they would do something like this, most of the boys answered a sheepish, "I don't know...." I confronted one young man about this activity and tried to explain the dangers of this behavior and how it could lead to infection and all sorts of complications. He promised me that he would stop. Unfortunately, he didn't stop soon enough because the next weekend he ended up in the hospital with an infection creeping up his arm. This was a scary situation. He was so embarrassed when he returned to school that he could barely speak to me after that.

As difficult as it may be, parents must be patient during this time and have a firm set of expectations that you want your child to follow. As teens enter high school, however, they are able make better decisions and chart their territory.

What's Next:

1. Talk to your child about the changes that they are going through mentally and physically.
2. Try to have reasonable expectations for your children during this time.
3. Have your child journal about how they are feeling.
4. Set up an appointment with your child's pediatrician so that the doctor can discus things with your child as well.

THE ROLE OF SLEEP

"Sleep deprivation is physically miserable and creatively cathartic, as internal landscapes rise up from their dormant ashes." ~ Jaeda DeWalt

Another issue of concern during the teen years is sleep, or the lack of it. During puberty, many systems are changing within the body. Sleep is one of those systems that is shifted during adolescence. Many middle school and high school children are not getting the recommended amount of sleep each night. Throw in the additional stress of maintaining grades, fitting in, and social activities, it's no wonder that kids are not sleeping well at night. Research has indicated that a lack of sleep can lead to irritability, poor focus, and difficulty learning just to name a few. The American Academy of Sleep Medicine has recommended that children ages 6-12 years should regularly sleep 9-12 hours per day and teenagers up to age eighteen should sleep 8-10 hours per day.

Data analyzed by the CDC from the 2015 Youth Risk Behavior survey indicated that youth ages 6-12 who reported sleeping less than nine hours were considered to not be getting enough sleep. Teenagers between the ages of 13-18 who reported sleeping less than eight hours were also considered to not be getting enough sleep.

In my many conversations over the years with middle school and high school students, many have indicated they do not get enough sleep or sleep well each night. In some cases, these teens are filled with worry about grades and exams. Others are dealing with relationships with friends. More recently, students are on social media. Some students indicate that they fall asleep with no problem but wake up at some point and cannot fall back to sleep. When I asked students roughly what time they go to bed, many students mention that it's between midnight and 1:00 a.m. This is much too late for school that starts at 7:45 a.m.

Years ago, I encountered one such student. Brad's parents were concerned that his grades were dropping, and he seemed unmotivated. I called Brad in to talk to him. He was well–liked and a good-natured kid. I finally got around to asking him if he slept well at night. He said, "Oh no, I don't sleep well at all."

I asked, "What do you do then?"

"I get up and go down to the basement and skateboard!"

I couldn't believe what he was telling me. His parents had no idea that he was getting up in the middle of the night. When I shared this information with Brad's mother, she looked at me in disbelief. She decided to take Brad to see his pediatrician. As it turned out, Brad had a sleeping disorder. He started medication and things began to improve. From that day on, as I meet with students who are having difficulties, I always ask them about their sleeping habits.

Some school systems have considered pushing back the start times for high schools. Many schools start as early as 7:00 a.m. A later start time could help those sleep deprived teens. As the studies indicate, sleep is very important, and lack of it for teens can lead to some of the anxiety and depression that kids are facing. In a 2010 study, James Gangwisch, PhD, of Columbia University in New York, noted that in addition to depression, adolescents with later bedtimes also had a greater risk of having suicidal thoughts. Dr. Gangwisch went on to state that the study "lends support to the idea that short sleep duration can be a risk factor for depression as opposed to simply being a symptom of depression." A study of 16,000 teenagers, grades 7-12, found that adolescents with bedtimes set at midnight or later were 24% more likely to suffer from depression than those with bedtimes of 10:00 p.m. or earlier. Teenagers with later bedtimes also were more likely to have suicidal thoughts. Depression and poor sleep habits go hand in hand, but sleep difficulties are usually seen as a symptom of depression, not a cause, says Dr. Gangwisch.[1]

As school systems evaluate their start times for high school students it may be important to examine later start times. In some high schools, upper classmen can set up their schedule so that they have a late arrival. A late arrival allows the student to have a free period during first period. This gives the student the opportunity to sleep in a little later.

What's Next:

1. Talk to your teen about healthy sleep habits and set a regular bedtime for your middle schooler.
2. Take electronic devices away from your teen before bedtime.
3. Have your teen end screen time an hour before bed.
4. Give your child an alarm clock so they don't have the excuse of needing their phone as an alarm.

THE ROLE OF SPORTS

Do you know what my favorite part of the game is? The opportunity to play. ~ Mike Singletary

One of the activities that can help teens develop healthy patterns is being involved in sports. Middle school is often the time when students can participate in school sports. Keeping children active during this time is very important. Some of the benefits of playing a sport are improved physical and mental health. According to Yael Klein, content writer for Evolve Treatment Centers, sports participation helps the body to release cortisol, which reduces stress. Endorphins are also released which is the bodies' natural feel-good chemicals. Sports participation can lead to better grades as well. Students must keep up their grades to be eligible to play a sport. Many coaches will have designated times where the teams' study together before practices. This is helpful because the students have a routine that can assist them with keeping up with their work.

Another important aspect of sports participation is the creation of a village. Deb Johnson, aka "DJ, The Sports Mom" and creator of The Professional Football Players Mothers' Association, states:

"Sports connect the village. It ties people and families together. Sports draw people in."

She also goes on to mention that sports can also help students work through mental health issues. Deb points out that sports can level the playing field. Everyone can have the opportunities in sports.

She does caution, however, that if there is too much stress and pressure to perform that this can lead to anxiety and depression. There must be a healthy balance of sports, community, and school participation. Teens can get overloaded at times and feel that they must participate in everything.

In speaking with Dr. Lisa Miller, Sports Psychology Professor at The Ohio State University, she states:

"Teens gain so many important outcomes from sports; friendships, mentorships, social support, exercise, guidance, nutrition information, and the ability to have experiences with diverse populations."

During my years as a middle school counselor, I worked with a student named Kevin. Kevin came from a family of high achievers. He had older sisters who were successful in school and doing well in college. Kevin was outgoing, friendly, and smart. He was on the swim team. In addition to that, he was a mentor to elementary students, and would read to them in the mornings before the middle school started. He was also on the superintendent's advisory council for the school district. He also took piano lessons once a week. Kevin came in to talk to me one day and I could tell something was bothering him, but he could not articulate what he was feeling. After a while he finally admitted to me that he was feeling overwhelmed and wasn't sure how to let go of some of his activities. He was worried about letting people down. We talked about which of his activities he felt comfortable backing away from. We brainstormed some possibilities, but he decided not to give up anything. I think he just felt better being able to talk about it.

As I have continued to work on this book, I have had the pleasure of interviewing and talking to many individuals about the complexities of being a teenager in today's world. I recently had a conversation with my colleague, Felicha Smith, who is also a school counselor regarding the journey that she and her teenage son, Jaden were on when he struggled with issues of anxiety and depression. Jaden, a good high school baseball player began to struggle. Here is their story:

I have been a school counselor for almost fourteen years and often reveal how much the profession has changed over the years. When I first started in the field back in 2004, I came fresh out of graduate school ready to counsel students into the real world! Little did I know, I was at the beginning stages of what counseling has now become. I was in no way trained in this area and had no background experience. I was out of my league. All I wanted to do was guide students in helping them make decisions for life after high school. As the years went on and mental health issues with teens was on the rise, I quickly had to grasp that this was my new reality. At first, I couldn't understand why some of my students suffered the way they did or how open and freely they talked about it. These were kids that grew up in affluent neighborhoods, who came from two parent homes, could afford nice family vacations, and were set up to go to college. What could they have problems with? Their lives seemed perfect...at least that is what I thought looking from the outside.

As an adult and working in the counseling field I had to try and navigate this new world of dealing with students who were suffering from a wide range of mental health issues, such as anxiety, depression, and ADHD (Attention, Deficit, Hyperactivity Disorder). I saw how students suffered from so many things and felt like no one understood them and how it ultimately consumed their lives.

I found myself getting better at being able to recognize certain mental illnesses and inadvertently learning how to help my students cope and/or know when they needed to be referred to outside therapy. It's grueling, emotionally draining, but oddly enough satisfying when I was able to really help a student through a tough time. So, I thought I had it figured out after many years. Fast forward to having my own family. Like I mentioned before, I thought my husband and I provided what would be needed so our kids would be healthy and happy. Not just physically healthy, but mentally also. My son Jaden, who is now 17 years old, had been playing baseball since he was five years old. He had a special talent. He was a tall, athletic, chiseled, African American boy that stood out since we were in a sport that is primarily dominated by Caucasian kids. In awe of his talent, people began to notice Jaden and came up to ask us, "Is that your son?" Proudly, we would say yes! In our minds, we felt our son was on his way to secure a scholarship to play collegiate baseball. As Jaden got older, we began to notice a change. He started to struggle with the mechanics of baseball and the once home run hitter was now not able to hit a ball! We couldn't understand why. My husband would work countless hours with him. We got him the necessary training we thought he needed. So, what was going on?

The joy of watching my son play began to dwindle as we continued to watch cringe worthy performances. I also began to notice that when Jaden did poorly, he would retreat to the back of the dugout to the point where he became nonexistent. I would go through a wide range of emotions from frustrated, puzzled, worried, to downright just sad for him. After each game, my husband would have the "talk." It was a scene that played out where my husband would question him, and my son would fumble to find an explanation. I slowly began to see his spirit being sucked away. I still had a hard time grasping what was happening because I thought my child was one of "those" kids that had all that he needed by growing up much more privileged than my husband and me.

June 15, 2020. I remember the day like it was yesterday. It was just another day where Jaden did not do well. This day, his stepsister happened to be at the game and asked if he could ride home with her. Reluctantly, we said yes, as my husband and I were eager to have the "talk." As soon as we got home, Jaden asked if he could write down what he was feeling, and we could too. In my mind, I already thought I knew what I was going to say, but we went ahead with the plan. After what seemed to be an agonizing amount of time, Jaden brings us his letter. It was two full pages, front and back of small writing. At first, I was a bit annoyed. As I read the letter, I felt my heart drop into my stomach and tears began to run down my face. My son had been in a dark place for a very long time. His self-esteem, along with what we now know was performance related anxiety had crippled him for all these years. Looking back, we missed obvious signs. Change in behavior, lack of caring for himself, and grades beginning to decline. We thought he just needed to train harder, focus more, believe in himself and things would get better.

I immediately put on my counselor hat and thought about what I did while working with families that were experiencing similar things. I had him meet with his pediatrician who diagnosed him and placed him on medication to help reduce his anxiety. I also felt he needed more and found a counselor that he could work with remotely since we were still in pandemic. Jaden worked with his counselor intensively for almost six months. It was unbelievable the growth and change we began to see with the interventions we put in place. We knew it would not be an *overnight fix, but through patience, hard work, and consistency Jaden was changing by gaining the necessary tools to do so.*

Changing who we are is an ever-evolving process and what I learned from being a parent and going through this experience, was that mental health issues can affect anyone. Never in a million years did I think my son would be going through this and I realized that we spent so much time trying to fix the physical aspects of him, that we unknowingly neglected to examine his mental state. Mental health issues are so prevalent amongst our youth and no matter how much experience you think you have; it is so important to listen to your children and be diligent about recognizing signs of any behavioral changes. The one thing I regret, is not knowing sooner that Jaden was struggling, therefore I could have gotten him the help that he needed.

Here's Jaden's story in his own words:

Growing up in a black household, mental health and awareness is not something that comes to the forefront. Which for most parents nowadays is not their fault as they were typically raised in that same way. My whole life, I have been playing baseball and I consider myself a good player but underneath my talent and success, there has always been a growing feeling of doubt and uncertainty about myself. After a while, this really affected my confidence which caused me to have low self-esteem. I really did not like the way my self-esteem took over my overall being so with the help of my parents, we found a life coach named Chris P Austin. With his assistance, I have honestly found key tips and strategies on Becoming My Best self that translates through baseball and my outside life. This truly helped me get out of my shell and explore my potential to the fullest extent. So now I am on my Varsity Baseball team and Swim Team Captain which have been results of my efforts to change my self-esteem. This is my story which is just the beginning, I am not fully there yet but progress is everything.[1] - Jaden Griffin, 17

It is important to recognize the pros and cons of children playing sports. As a family you should decide if you (or your child for that matter) wants to play on school teams and or club teams. Are you thinking/hoping that your child will play at the collegiate level? According to Dr. Lisa Miller:

"Parents can offer and support a variety of activities to their children to see what their child finds most motivating. Parents need to recognize the impact that leader(coach) has on a child; If the child may need another opportunity to try that activity with a different leader. On the opposite side, are children picking an activity based on the inspiration of one coach. It's important to have children try a variety of things."

All things must be considered, but most importantly, is your child having fun, making friends, and enjoying the activity? If you cannot answer yes to all these questions, then maybe it's time to reevaluate their choices as it relates to organized sports.

<u>What's Next:</u>

1. Explore a variety of sports/activities with your child.
2. Encourage participation in sports or other activities, but make sure there is a healthy balance.

HELPING CHILDREN CREATE THEIR LEGACIES - FINDING PURPOSE AND PASSION: WHY NOT START NOW?

The two most important days in your life are the day you were born and the day you find out why. ~ Mark Twain

At an early age, parents need to foster children's purpose, passions, and gifts in their children. In my work with a career counselor, Mary Lynne Musgrove, she taught us that everyone has an *internal job description*. It is the job of parents and educators to help children discover this. Mary Lynne suggests that the internal job description is where an individual's *gifts* intersect with their *passions*. What are gifts? Gifts are those things that we naturally do better than others. It's a skill or something that an individual does with little effort. She believed that gifts are things that an individual is born with. I'm sure you can think of things that just come very easily to you and take little effort for you to do. Some individuals are gifted at public speaking. Others at baking or cooking. These activities come naturally to them.

What are passions? Passions are those things that we truly enjoy, and we lose track of time when we are involved in those activities. For example, I have a passion for tennis. I could play for hours if my body would allow me to!

Some people love to garden and could spend all day planting, weeding, etc. Others love quilting and crocheting. Passions don't necessarily have to be things we do well. I certainly am not the best tennis player, but I enjoy tennis and could improve my game the more I play. With children, we need to observe at an early age what kinds of things hold their attention, and what things they enjoy. Observing these things could be key to what children might do later in life. Observing gifts and passions gives an idea of a child's strengths. Is the child a strong leader among his friends, does he/she like to spend time alone reading, or are they one to be the life of the party? All these questions and observations can give us clues that could lead to future possibilities. When children have a strong sense of who they are in the world and understand their gifts and passions they can begin to create their legacies.

Reflection is another key to the puzzle. As children experience various activities, we need to ask key questions such as "what did you like about this activity? Is this something you could see yourself doing in the future? What other experiences would you like to have?" A great reflection activity is to have children write down the things they enjoyed over summer break or on a family vacation. What did they enjoy? What didn't they enjoy and why? These types of open-ended questions can give parents clues to what their children are thinking about or enjoy.

Mary Lynne Musgrove suggested that we help children create an entrepreneurial spirit. "An entrepreneurial spirit is a mindset. It's an attitude and approach to thinking that actively seeks out change, rather than waiting to adapt to change. It's a mindset that embraces critical questioning, innovation, service, and continuous improvement." When we equip students with an entrepreneurial spirit, they can confidently say, "I'm not sure what career is out there for me, but these are the skills and abilities I possess." When children have confidence in their gifts, passions, skills, and abilities, they are better equipped to explore possibilities.

As mentioned before, parents want their children to be happy. But what does that mean? Sometimes that happiness comes with conditions. "I want them to be happy as long as they get A's. I want them to be happy as long as they play the violin, I want them to be happy as long as they find a job. What does it mean to be happy? How do we help kids find happiness and begin to create their legacies? Part of helping children create their legacies is by helping them find their purpose and passion. Some people may think that trying to help kids create a legacy is too much. Legacy is something that adults strive for. It's too early for them to think about legacy. Children can start thinking about legacy while they are young, so they can create a vision and then begin to find the happiness the parents so desperately want them to have.

What is a legacy? Webster's definition states that legacy is *something transmitted by or received from an ancestor or predecessor or from the past.* Legacy is about life and learning. Learning from the past, living in the present and building for the future. A few years ago, I asked a senior high school student, Todd, what he thought legacy meant. Todd stated that legacy is the "mark you leave on other people's lives. The impact, inspiration. What other people remember about your relationships and how it changes others." Todd at the time wasn't sure what he wanted to do, but he wants to be a leader that inspires others and has a service component. He developed this in high school. He has had faith, unconditional love, and support and he wants to give back. For those who don't have that support, Todd suggested that students have to be the change they want to see.

His sister, Terri, believes legacy is about how we accomplish things. Accomplishments mean nothing unless we can help and impact the lives of others. Terri discovered in her junior year that she wanted to be an athletic trainer or physical therapist. She loved serving others and having faith, always showing a love for God for people. She believes we must lead by example, sacrificing time for others and investing time, not for selfish reasons." These amazing twins were involved in service during high school and were always finding ways to give to others.

When students learn to give to others and be of service to others, it strengthens their self-confidence and gives them the courage to step outside of their comfort zone and try other things.

I had the opportunity to speak with another senior, Joey. Joey believes that legacy is what people see when you're not active anymore. What you leave behind for others to build on. Joey has known since first grade that he wanted to work in ecology. His family's frequent trips to Florida helped fuel his interest in nature, the ocean, birds, etc. He thought the dolphins were cool and understood that they are as smart as humans. His parents introduced him to the outdoors. Joey feels that kids have to do what they need to do to put them in a place to do what they want to do. Kids have to find that out for themselves, what they enjoy. It has to come from within. Sometimes parents pushing children toward something can be more of a burden to the child. Middle school is the time that students need to start figuring out what they want to do. In middle school, Joey's teacher, pushed Joey to take honors English for high school. Joey admits at first that he didn't want to, but once he took the course, he wanted to perfect everything he did from that point on. He had internalized the drive. Joey wants to be remembered as hardworking, honest, and humble.

Parents must create opportunities for children at a young age to experience many things. As children have a variety of experiences, they can begin to figure out what things they enjoy. Another way to give children these experiences is through community service. People often comment that middle school children are self-absorbed and rarely think about others. I believe that is true in some cases. When children are given the opportunity to think about someone other than themselves, they usually rise to the occasion.

Students who seem to have purpose and passion often do better in school because they have a focus and a vision for their future. They are less likely to be involved in drugs and alcohol and have a better sense of themselves and their overall identity. Students who are connected to school through an activity or a sport often do better as well. Some kids struggle to fit in at school and can become disengaged and often fail. Over the last few years, I have noticed a trend among some of the high school students. For example, Chad. Chad struggled to fit in during his middle school years and things didn't change much when he got to high school. Chad found reasons to leave the classroom and was always in the halls. Chad did very little homework and often instigated fights with others. By his senior year,

Chad was placed at an alternative high school for part of the day. As his senior year went on, I noticed some changes in Chad. He was more pleasant in the hallways. He was going to class more often and was not getting in trouble. I asked him one day what had changed. He said "I'm working now. I have to be nice to the customers and be responsible."

I believe that working does change a student. He or she must think about someone other than themselves and they have to be reasonably responsible. I was surprised at the changes Chad had made but it made sense. I have seen other students grow and mature when they started working. Working does several things for kids; it gives them a sense of responsibility, they become a part of something bigger than themselves, they feel a sense of accomplishment, a sense of purpose, and it often takes them out of their comfort zones to learn new things. Part of growing is being stretched and taken out of our comfort zones. As mentioned before, some parents are so fearful of their child failing (at anything), that they won't allow their children to step out of their comfort zone. As Joey stated earlier, he was not sure about taking an honors English class in high school. When he took the class, he realized he could do the work and accomplish great things. He was stretched out of his comfort zone, and he grew because of it. Joey chose not to be average. John Maxwell states in his book, *The 15 Laws of Invaluable Growth:*

"Being average is to take up space for no purpose; to take the trip through life, but never pay the fare; to return no interest for God's investment in you."[1]

I would imagine that every parent wants their child to be great and not average. In my life, service to others and the community was modeled in my family. My mother was a school nurse, and my father was the director of physical therapy at The Ohio State University. My parents were community-minded individuals. My dad would often provide home health care services at home to some of his patients. My brother and I would often tag along when he went to a patient's home. My father would provide these patients with crutches, wheelchairs, and other devices that would make them more comfortable at home. He did this free of charge. Sometimes he would get the equipment back, and other times he did not. My dad kept extra items on hand that he would loan to people as needed. Our basement looked like a medical supply company, with walkers, crutches, wheelchairs, etc. On occasion, we would see some of his patients after they recovered, at a restaurant or store. These individuals would thank my father for helping them recover. It was such a good feeling to see my father receive these compliments.

My mother was a member of a service organization that awarded scholarships to local urban high school students. This organization held a fashion show/luncheon every year as a fundraiser. I enjoyed attending this event with my mother. We would dress up and I would host a table of my friends at the luncheon. This event raised a lot of money for the group. My mother enjoyed being a part of this group and giving to others. My parents never made a big deal about what they were doing, but as I reflect, I know they had a sense of pride in what they were doing and that was modeled for me. Laura Wilkinson, Olympic diver in an interview when asked about her drive and determination recently said "When you are called to do something and you are passionate about it, you want to be all in."

What's Next:

1. Volunteer at homeless shelters and church organizations in your neighborhood.
2. Have your child find an older adult in the neighborhood that they can help.

THE FAMILY AS A SYSTEM

Family is not an important thing. It's everything. ~ Michael J. Fox

My favorite class in graduate school was Family Systems Therapy. Family systems therapy is a form of psychotherapy that supports people in resolving conflicts that exist within a family unit. All members of the family contribute to the dynamic of whether the family is functioning in a healthy or dysfunctional way.[1]

This makes sense to me. A family unit is really like a machine or a system. When one part of the family or "system" is not working, then this can damage or hamper the rest of the family. I have used this analogy with many students I have worked with. Just like with a car if the spark plugs go bad, the car will not run. Some parts of a car may be damaged, but not completely broken. The car may run but not very efficiently. The same is true with families. A family can still function if part of the system is not working, but not very effectively. It is typically the children that suffer in these situations. In some cases, the child could be the one causing the system to not function well. Parents can have disputes on parenting strategies. Children could be dealing with mental health or school issues. In these cases, parents must get on the same page as to how to deal with these circumstances. Kids need to know that they have a role in the family or system. Their roles are to go to school, work hard, and do things, like chores or other things that parents want them to do. Jessica Lahey states, in her book *The Gift of Failure*:

Children are starved for responsibility and a role within the family, and all the jockeying for power, and the mischief that arises when their hands are idle, stem from our failure to give our kids a clear way to contribute to the family's well-being. Kids thrive on our expectations, and they flourish when given responsibilities of their own and the education they need to carry them out successfully."[2]

In many situations when parents would consult with me about their children, I would ask them if their child had responsibilities at home. Often the parent would reluctantly say no. The comment was always, "I just want my child to focus on school." I would counter and tell the parent that children have a role at home to play as well. The role they play at home helps them to feel like part of the family unit.

In one of my earlier years as a middle school counselor, I had a mother who asked to speak with me about her daughter. She came to the meeting, exasperated, and frustrated. She told me that her daughter was having difficulty with her hygiene. She would not take showers or baths. I was incredulous. Her daughter, at school was smart, outgoing, and generally, a good student. She begged me to have a conversation with her daughter. I did have a conversation with her daughter and explained that she has a role in her family and that role was to go to school, take care of herself, and help the family in general. I think the student understood, and she couldn't give me a reason for why she was refusing to shower. A few weeks later this students' mom called me and said that things had gotten better at home.

Kids need to know and understand that they have a role to play in the family and that their role is important. Kids need to feel like they are part of the family unit and have things they can contribute. I have friends whose middle school and high school kids love to cook. They make sure that their child has an opportunity to show off their skills by cooking on occasion. Other kids may enjoy working in the yard or helping at the grocery store. Any opportunity for kids to be involved in the family activities will allow them to feel a sense of accomplishment and confidence.

Kids can also feel connected to their families through stories that parents share. Connectedness occurs when parents share stories about things they did when they were growing up; not the story that they walked five miles uphill in the snow to go to school, but meaningful stories about their childhood. What kinds of struggles did you overcome? What did you enjoy doing as a child? Who was your best friend? What did you get in trouble for? When parents share those types of stories with their children, it can connect them to their child's experiences.

My mother was the oldest child in her family with four younger brothers. She would share stories about how she had to take care of them and the kinds of things they did as a family when she was a child. When I was growing up and we had family gatherings, I saw my uncles as larger than life. They were cool, accomplished men who I still look up to today. They would talk about how my mother took care of them and some of the mischievous stuff they did as little boys.

My father used to share stories about growing up in Kentucky and the type of jobs he had in high school and college. Some of the stories were funny. Sometimes kids don't want to hear the stories that their parents share, but as they get older, they will remember and cherish those stories. Sharing stories and demonstrating your family values will eventually resonate with your children and help them to feel a sense of belonging in the family.

What's Next:

1. Establish chores and routines for children at an early age.
2. Have a schedule and make a chart of the refrigerator.
3. Children must complete their tasks before planning other activities.
4. Share stories with your children.

My uncles and me (circa 1974)

EXPOSURE AND EXPERIENCE CAN EXPAND POTENTIAL

~ Kathy Starks

During my years as a counselor at Perry Middle School, we hosted an annual career day for our seventh and eighth-grade students. This practice was taking place before I started working there and continued when I arrived. Our seventh-grade students spent the day out of the building shadowing individuals (not their parents), in a variety of professions and careers. The students had a packet of questions they had the ask the person they shadowed to find out details about the career or job. The eighth-grade students stayed at school and a variety of professionals came in and presented to the students about their careers. The students were able to choose four career areas they were interested in learning about throughout the afternoon. During the morning, the students attended their classes on an abbreviated schedule.

The shadowing day and the career fair exposed students to new possibilities and activities they had not thought about before. The students in both grade levels loved this day. The seventh graders especially came back to school the next day excited, energized, and wanting to do it again. Some of the careers' students thought they might enjoy changed when they saw someone working in that profession. Other students had a desire for a certain path and their desires were solidified by their actual exposure to the career.

We must provide opportunities for students to have such experiences to expand their view of the world of work. My favorite story is about a young man named Eli. Here is Elis's story:

You may think that choosing your career at just fifteen years old may seem a tad bit premature, but it wasn't in my case. Ever since being a little boy I always admired firefighters and had an obsession with their big red trucks. When I was in middle school, I didn't really know what I wanted to do in high school or college and was just going through the motions, "playing school." Ms. Starks reached out to me and let me know if I was interested, she could set me up to shadow at our local fire department. I thought, what harm could it do? Little did I know that right then and there set the path for my foreseeable future.

Through going to shadow at the fire department, I discovered that the fire service was the right career choice for me. I spent the next 3 years going to that firehouse every month to ride along on the trucks and "live the life" of a firefighter. I found out that being a firefighter was a lot more than just lights and sirens and big infernos. Through doing the ride a long's I became much more comfortable talking to adults, more flexible with last minute changes, and I saw a purpose to all of the work of being in school, a light at the end of the tunnel as they call it. Our community is blessed to have a vocational school which I chose to attend during junior and senior year of high school.

The vocational school brought it all together. I went to my primary high school half of the day and the other half I spent learning about the career I wanted to pursue. The career center is a two year program which allows you to obtain all the certifications you need to become a firefighter/EMT when you graduate. It is a mixture of classroom learning paired with a lot of hands-on, real-world training. There are so many programs to choose from and there is most certainly a program tailored to anyone's interests. During my time at the career center, I spent almost two years at another local firehouse doing ride-time.

The firehouse mentioned is what absolutely sealed the deal for me personally. Everyone I met was incredibly willing to teach and help me throughout school. Being able to respond to emergencies and see first-hand what I was training for made school a lot easier. It came full circle, seeing what I had only been taught about in the classroom gave me a better grasp over many various concepts. After graduating, this same firehouse hired me as a firefighter, and it is still where I am employed today.

I am in a paramedic program, which is at a local college. It isn't the traditional "college experience" but it is furthering my education so that I can better serve the communities I work in. College may not be for everyone, but you can absolutely make a living doing work you enjoy. Find a job you enjoy doing and you will never have to work a day in your life.[1] ~ Elijah Malench (2021)

Eli Malench, Spring 2021

Many children have no idea what they want to do or what they enjoy. As parents and educators, we must give kids opportunities to explore a variety of things. We must provide opportunities at school and home for children to explore new possibilities. Parents can plan outings to local areas of interest, take children on day trips, and visits places of interest. The more opportunities children have to explore, the better equipped they will be to make decisions later about their future career path. My young friend Nia believes she was fortunate to have wonderful exposure to extended family members who gave her the opportunity to see successful adults around her and instilled in her the belief that she could be just as successful. Parents must create opportunities for children at an early age to experience many things.

Another way to give children these experiences is through community service. People often comment that middle school children are self-absorbed and rarely think about others. I believe that is true in some cases. When children are given the opportunity to think about someone other than themselves, they usually rise to the occasion. During my time at Perry Middle School, we facilitated a club called IMPACT (I Make Powerful Actions and Contributions Today, and Tomorrow). The IMPACT group was for eighth-grade students. They would organize bake sales and other fundraising activities throughout the year. During the Christmas season, the students would take the money they raised and shop for young children at a local daycare that was in an economically disadvantaged area of town. Before Christmas, the students would volunteer at the daycare, reading and playing with the children and getting to know them. During the holiday season, students would pair up and with the children's Christmas list in hand and go shopping to fulfill the children's wishes. They would come back to school and wrap the gifts. Right before the holiday break, we would deliver the gifts to the children. Our eighth-grade students were so moved by the responses of the preschoolers. This activity changed many of the eight-grade students and they were excited about giving to others and thinking about others.

The IMPACT group also went to a local assisted living community and decorated the facility for the Christmas holidays. The students would put together Christmas trees, string lights, and make holiday cards for the residents. The teachers would often see an entirely new side of a student during this time. Students who sometimes seemed unmotivated in class, blossomed during this activity. They were highly engaged and wanted to do anything they could to work with the residents at the facility. It seemed that the students were engaged because of intrinsic motivation or value of these activities. The students weren't getting extra credit for participating in the group, or any other accolades. They were simply participating because they wanted to.

In my last few years of working at the high school, I have helped facilitate two wonderful activities that have allowed kids to have exposure to various careers. In the fall we host a ninth-grade career fair. We invite a variety of professionals to come in and set up tables to showcase their careers/professions. The students can walk around and engage with these professionals, ask questions, and make connections with adults outside of their normal routine. The students are also encouraged to inquire about shadowing someone in a field that might interest them. The feedback from most of the students is positive. Students learn a little bit about a career they never thought of.

In addition to the career fair, the high school counselors host a job fair for the juniors and senior students. We have created a list of potential employers who are looking to hire students for the summer or even permanently. The students are asked to dress up and bring their resumes. Over the last few years, the job fair has been a great success. The students can practice their interviewing skills and make connections. Some students walk away from this experience with opportunities for potential employment and exposure to many other employers. Some of the students are uncomfortable approaching someone they don't know and inquiring about their businesses, but after speaking with a few employers, the students are more comfortable and relaxed and can engage with the professionals. This experience is teaching students networking skills. The students can interact with many professionals. They can collect business cards and contact information that could be used later. Many students walked away from this experience stating that it was the best thing they had done to get them ready for life after high school. The value of this type of exposure is immeasurable. It gets kids out of their comfort zones, which then allows them to have more confidence in the future.

Involving children in activities where they can give back and think about others is very meaningful and can help lead children to more positive ways of thinking and interacting. When we can engage in a cause that's bigger than ourselves and participate collaboratively with others, it changes our mindset and attitude. Students need to be provided with opportunities to do just that. Parents can take children to a local food bank or pantry to deliver food or take old clothing to a homeless shelter. These activities let children know that others are in worse situations and allows them to be a bit more compassionate.

Thomas Worthington High School has a community service club. The service club completely furnishes an apartment or house for a family transitioning out of homelessness. The students, along with teacher leaders, Judi and Bob Galasso, search for bed frames, mattresses, kitchen supplies, and furniture for the homes. Community members donate many items. Items that aren't donated are purchased by students in the group and sometimes their parents. The Welcome Home group as it's called also has received monetary donations from community members, which has allowed the group to purchase items for the homes. On one Saturday a month, the students load up the U-Haul truck with items for a particular home, and head out to the site. Mrs. Galasso gets information from the Homeless Families Foundation regarding how many members are in the family including the number of children. Earlier in the week, Mrs. Galasso is given the address of the home. The students carpool and meet at the home.

Once the truck is unloaded with all the items for that home, the kids get to work organizing the children's bedrooms, decorating the bathrooms, etc. Some of the adults that participate, work to organize the kitchen. Within a couple of hours, the home is completely furnished with pictures on the walls and furniture in every room. It looks like someone has been living there for years. Not only is the house transformed, but so are the kids that are involved in this activity. The students come away from this activity with a sense of purpose and pride that they were able to help someone in need. The Worthington School district is an upper middle class community. When I talked with Judi and Bob Galasso about the experiences the students had, they said that the community service students were surprised that just twenty minutes away from their community, people were living very different lives. Some of the students had never traveled to these lower socioeconomic parts of town and did not realize they were not that far from their suburban community.

Another way children can find purpose and passion is by understanding multiple intelligences. The multiple intelligences theory was developed by Howard Gardner in his 1983 book, *Frames of Mind*. This theory suggests that human intelligence can be divided into eight abilities. These intelligences include musical-rhythmic, visual spatial, verbal linguistic, bodily kinesthetic, interpersonal, intrapersonal, and naturalist. There are multiple intelligence surveys that students can take to give them and idea of what areas they excel in and what areas may still need to be developed. In 2009, Gardner suggested that existential and moral intelligences be included as well. Below are two diagrams that depict the multiple intelligences:

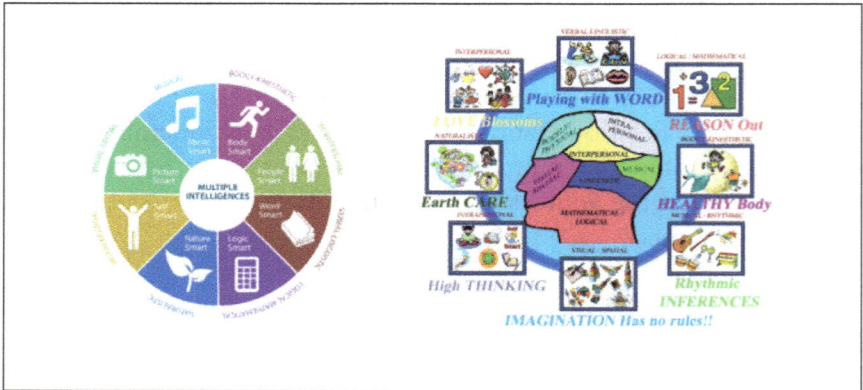

2, 3

Parents can observe young children to see which intelligence their child seems to excel in. Is it easy for your child to strike up conversations with new people? Does your child enjoy playing multiple sports and participating in physical activities? Are math and logical concepts easy for your child to understand? Observing these things in your children can give you an idea of their strengths and weaknesses in each of these areas.

What's next:

1. Expose your children to a variety of experiences.
2. Have children volunteer in the community
3. Have children volunteer or shadow in a career field they might be interested in.
4. Have children take the Multiple Intelligence survey.

RESILIENCE

"Life is not the way it's supposed to be. It's the way it is. The way you cope with it makes the difference." ~ Virginia Satir

In an earlier chapter, I talked about enabling behaviors. Parents often don't want their children to fail or to suffer the consequences of life's circumstances. As mentioned before, those children will have a much harder time making it through life. Ideally, parents want their children to be happy, healthy, and successful. But they will need to learn resilience for that to happen. Resilience is the ability to overcome difficult situations and move forward in life. Madeline Levine states in her book *The Price of Privilege: How Parental Pressures and Material Advantage are Creating a Generation of Disconnected and Unhappy Kids*:

"A child cannot possibly develop resilience when parents are constantly at his side, interfering with the development of autonomy, self-management, and coping skills."

She goes on to further state:

"The adolescent who reaches down inside himself and finds that he is capable of working through a difficult problem is at a tremendous advantage, both psychologically and practically, over the adolescent who depends on others to 'fix' things for them."[1]

Resilience refers to the ability to cope with adversity in a healthy way and move forward. People often comment that children are resilient. They can bounce back from anything. Carol Taylor, a trauma/resilience consultant, contends that we must teach young people to be resilient, that children are not naturally resilient. Carol believes that resilience is achieved because of connectedness. Children have to be connected to a parent, teacher, or coach. This connectedness is what equips individuals with the tools to cope with adversity. Resiliency can be built through loving relationships. So many young people have overcome a myriad of things to be successful people: homelessness, physical and mental abuse, and substance abuse. They often make it through these situations because of the connectedness they have with someone in their lives.

Over the years I have witnessed so many students overcoming what might seem like insurmountable odds; the death of a sibling or parent, car accidents, drug and alcohol abuse just to name a few. As the students are going through these situations many of them are surrounded by many caring adults and great peer groups. They seem to rise to the challenges and forge ahead. In the cases where students can't seem to overcome obstacles, they have a small support network, and in many cases that network does not include a parent. I am reminded of a few students whose parents were so disengaged and struggling with their own issues that they had little emotional or physical ability to help their child. In those cases, the student was not connected to many people at school either. Those students typically gave up and eventually dropped out of school.

Before resilience can be developed, I believe that the child needs to have a strong sense of self efficacy. Psychologist Albert Bandura originally proposed self-efficacy. It is a personal judgement of how well or poorly a person can cope with a given situation based on the skills they have and the circumstances they face. Dr. Kirsten Smith believes that summer camps give kids the opportunity to practice resilience. Camps provide kids the chance to try new things and meet new people in a safe environment away from home where they can gain some independence.

Some students have not had to be resilient yet and are woefully unprepared for the next steps to adulthood. I recall a senior I worked with named Terry, or TJ for short. TJ's fun personality gained him many friends. A relatively good student, TJ appeared to have it all together. The truth was that he was a scared little boy. His fears stemmed from the idea that he might not be successful in college. This fear had him in a state of avoidance and shutdown mode. Vetted to run track, he had not applied to any university, followed through with any of the coaches who had reached out to him, or even scheduled an appointment with his school counselor to help him navigate everything. Terry was so used to being in the "bubble" of his high school environment that he had given little thought to his next steps. After talking with me he agreed to schedule a meeting with his counselor and started applying to various universities. He finally pulled everything together and plans to run track at a small university.

I recently spoke with Art Therapist Joan Zeller of Zeller and Associates regarding some of the issues she is seeing in her practice. She is noticing that kids today can't tolerate boredom. They don't know how to deal with it. They have to be on social media. Today's kids have not learned how to deal with solitude according to Zeller. For some of Zeller's clients, the pandemic of 2020 was a welcome relief. Her teen clients who suffer from anxiety and depression were happy to be at home not having to worry about social engagement. But after a while those same students were having more anxiety because they had to be alone with their own thoughts and feelings. According to Zeller, "When we are ok with being alone, we are more equipped to be with others." It seems to me that some teens today have not been given the opportunity to learn how to do this. Children can learn resilience by being alone and working out a variety of situations on their own without turning to social media or friends to help them resolve issues.

When I think about my teenage years, I am reminded of the time I tried out for the girl's tennis team at my high school. I have always loved tennis. My father introduced the sport to my brother and me during our summer trips to Bowling Green, Kentucky to visit my great-grandmother. My dad would take us to the campus of Western Kentucky University to play on the tennis courts there. I was probably thirteen or fourteen at the time. My brother didn't have much interest, but I enjoyed playing. I would ask friends to play with me at home. In the mid-seventies however, not too many African American kids were playing tennis. I would practice alone on backboards and concrete walls around town. I decided to try out for the high school team during my sophomore year. I knew how to play, how to keep score and I could keep the ball in play. Unfortunately, I did not make the team. I was devastated, but I didn't give up.

The coach at the time, who was also my social studies teacher, told me to keep playing and not to give up on the sport. I continued to play on my own and had a lesson or two. I decided to try out again my senior year and still did not make the team. Again, coach was encouraging and told me to keep playing because I could play as an adult and really enjoy myself. I never forgot what coach said. I signed up for tennis as one of my college electives and continued to play. After college I had a few friends who enjoyed playing and I started playing with them. I finally joined a tennis club in the early nineties after grad school and played on several ladies' teams and mixed doubles teams. I had the support of the coach and others to keep playing, and after all these years, I am now the junior varsity coach at the very school where I could not play when I was a student.

I didn't have parents who complained to the coach that I should be on the team, or that I deserved to be on the team. I had parents who knew I was upset, but also knew that I had to move on and handle my disappointment. Some parents have difficulty allowing the children to experience defeat, let downs, or heartbreak. I certainly understand that parents don't want their children to suffer, but through suffering comes strength and growth and knowledge of how to handle difficult situations when they arise again as adults.

Teachers can also create connectedness with students by sharing stories with their students. I believe that I have been successful as a school counselor because I have always been willing to share personal things with my students. As a middle school counselor, I facilitated classroom guidance activities. On the first day of the session, I would always share things with my students about where I grew up and the things I enjoyed. This allowed the students to feel more comfortable sharing things with me. The students were able to see me as human and not just an authority figure in the classroom. I let the students know that I struggled in middle school and had difficulty in high school as well. They could see that it's possible to overcome situations and be successful even if you do struggle at times.

One year I remember working with a student named Sharon. Sharon struggled with learning disabilities and didn't like school. When she was frustrated in the classroom, she would often run out of the class and hide in the bathroom. She had very few coping skills to manage her frustration. She had a strong sense of right and wrong and if things took place in her classes that she didn't agree with, she would get upset and leave the class. I would intervene on many of these occasions to calm her down. She was frustrated that she couldn't learn things as quickly as other students. In one of my conversations with her, I told her the story of another student that I knew who struggled as she did in school. This student had hearing loss and often missed what was taking place in the classroom but was too nervous to ask for help. This student had C's and D's in high school and was just an average student. I told Sharon that this student went on to college and struggled there as well, but eventually graduated. I shared that this student eventually became a school counselor, and that student was me!

She stared at me in disbelief and said, "You were that student who struggled?"

"Yes, Sharon, I was that student."

Sharon's entire attitude began to change. She started coming to see me on a more regular basis when she was frustrated in class instead of running into the bathroom. Sharon persevered through high school and has graduated. She overcame some obstacles and has become very resilient.

Personal stories have an impact. They allow others to hear your struggles and maybe even identify with you. The teachers who can identify and connect with students are usually the most successful and most well-liked teachers. In addition to teachers sharing stories with their children and students, we need to hear the students' stories.

Often students come into a classroom sullen, withdrawn, or disengaged. I know that most teachers would reach out and attempt to find out what's going on with that student. Sometimes, however, the teachers may not have the time or ability to do that with every student. When adults take the time to truly find out what is going on in the lives of the children that we interact with, it can create a bond that will allow the student to more open and give them more confidence. The more confidence a student has, the more resilient they can become.

A few years ago, I encountered a student that I wanted to get to know. His name was James. I would see James in the hallways, cursing, appearing angry, late to class, etc. One day I told him that I wanted to talk to him. His response was, "Why do you want to talk to me? Am I in trouble?" I told him that he was not in trouble, but I wanted to get to know him. I told him that he seemed angry and was always cursing in the hallway. I then said, "What's your story?"

James said, "What do you mean?"

I told him I wanted to know who he was. He told me that he didn't like the school and that when he needed help getting back on track the previous year after suffering a concussion in football, that only a couple of teachers were willing to help him. I told him that he was making it difficult for people to get to know him because his attitude was pushing people away. I told him a little bit about myself and where I grew up and that I had actually walked the same hallways that he was walking.

I know this sounds strange, but I literally could see and feel his walls of defensiveness coming down. James and I continued to talk for about an hour. He told me that his grades were good and that he wanted to be a psychologist. I told James that I could see him for the true person that he was and that he had the potential to be a leader. From that day forward, James would greet me in the hallway and stop to chat. He stopped cursing in the hallways, and in general, had a better attitude. He still had a few challenges along the way, but his overall demeanor changed drastically. James knew that I cared about him and that other adults in the building cared about him as well.

James has graduated now and is entering his third year of college.

Resiliency plays an important role as children attempt to resolve conflicts with peers and adults. Many times, the over-involved parents will try to intervene on behalf of their child and of course, ends up making things worse. On the occasions when I had students that were having disagreements with each other, there were a few times that the parents wanted to get involved and confront the parent of the other child. Those situations never worked out very well. I realized that it was better to let students handle their disagreements as much as possible and leave the adults out of it. On some occasions, I would bring students together in my office and I would leave so they could work out their issues. The students were grateful for the opportunity to just sit, talk, and resolve their issues. I recently spoke to an elementary principal who told me that they had to stop letting children play soccer during recess because so many parents called complaining that their child was being bullied, when in fact they were getting knocked down or tousled around during the soccer game. No real bullying was occurring.

Bullying and harassment situations, of course, are different and *may* need adult intervention if the child has made attempts to resolve the situation and was not able to. Allowing students to handle disagreements gives the students a level of confidence they would have never gained otherwise, and it enables them to be resilient during difficult situations. Allowing kids to handle situations with appropriate guidance will enable them to build self-confidence which will lead to resilience.

One of the strategies I love to use to help students in difficult situations is mediation. When I was working in the middle school, a select group of students were chosen to be student mediators. They along with the staff advisors went through a weekend of mediation training. The kids were taught how to run a mediation and how to engage with the students who were taking part in the mediation. This program was well-received by the staff and parents. So many situations were resolved with the student mediators that otherwise may have resulted in disciplinary actions. The student mediators gained a great deal of confidence, and the students who were brought to mediation were relieved that they were able to settle their disagreements without adult intervention.

Now that I am working at the high school level, I have been able to facilitate mediations between students, and between students and teachers. On several occasions, students have been upset about something that happened in one of their classes. Their default setting is "That teacher doesn't like me!" or "I don't want to go back to that class again." I have calmly sat down with the student and told them that they can't drop the class and we need to work out a solution with the teacher. It has been great to see the teacher and the student work through an issue and maintain the teacher-student relationship. This type of intervention is different than a parent getting involved in school issues. As the counselor, I am an impartial third party, willing to hear both sides. The student gains the confidence to speak up for themselves and the teacher can keep her relationship with the student intact. This is a win-win situation. Allowing kids to handle situations with appropriate guidance will enable them to build self-confidence, which can lead to resilience. Kids need to know that a supportive adult will be in their corner if they need them.

What's next:

1. Teach children how to ask for help when they need it.
2. Teach them how to problem solve. It will get easier each time.
3. Support your children through their struggle so they can learn resilience and confidence.
4. Model for children how to handle difficult situations and allow them to practice handling tough situations through role-playing.

High school graduation picture, 1977

PARENTING STYLES AND DISCIPLINE

If we don't shape our kids, they will be shaped by outside forces that don't care what shape our kids are in. ~Dr. Louise Hart

Over the years parents have asked my advice about how to discipline their children for a variety of infractions, ranging from not cleaning their rooms to being involved with drugs and alcohol. The parents who end up being the most successful in their discipline practices are firm, fair, and consistent. The discipline has to fit the crime, and parents need to have important conversations with their children when the misbehavior could lead to injury or self-harm. Consistency is very important when it comes to discipline. If you say to your child that they can't do something, then you need to mean it. Jessica Lahey said it best: There is nothing to be gained be idle threats, and everything to lose.[1]

A good example is when high school kids come home way past curfew and maybe have been drinking or smoking. I know you have heard about this scenario a million times. The child comes in at 2:00 am. Parents are sitting up worried to death because the child is not responding to text messages or phone calls and has turned their phone off. Immediately one of the parents goes into a tirade and yells at the child to go up to their room and that they are grounded for the next decade. This style usually doesn't work and is not realistic. I have had a few friends put themselves in "time-out" instead of their children. When their child has misbehaved, the parent doesn't discuss the issue right then. Instead, they take a time out to collect their thoughts and talk to their child when they have calmed down and can think more rationally. Whatever style of parenting and discipline is used it's important to understand that fairness and consistency are key.

Parenting styles have widely been written about over the years. Parenting styles fall into several categories: Authoritarian, Permissive, and Authoritative.

Authoritarian parents have an "it's my way or the highway" attitude. These parents believe that their children must behave and act appropriately at all times. These parents believe that they are always in control and can control their child's behavior. The problem with this style of parenting is that the children area afraid of their parents which can lead to depression and anxiety. In this type of parenting, love is conditional. These parents rarely praise their children for anything. Their belief is that good grades and good behavior are expected, so why should I praise them for that? This kind of thinking may be fine for younger children, but as kids reach adolescence, their need to experiment and find their own identity can spell trouble in the household. Madeline Levine writes:

"In adolescence, however, their homes can become war zones as rebellious teens are severely penalized for engaging is the kinds of healthy risk taking that are not sanctioned by authoritarian parents. This includes everything from divergent political views to occasional drug or alcohol experimentation."

I recall one such incident several years ago. John was a well-liked guy, but school was not his thing. In middle school, things got worse. He was hanging with the wrong crowd and not doing his schoolwork. He was seeing a private counselor to try to work things out. John's mother asked if I could also speak to her son so that he would have someone at school to talk with as well. I enjoyed talking with John. One on one, he seemed easy to talk to. He told me about his interests and some of his friends. Things drastically changed when I asked him about his father. He said, "I can't stand the guy." He puts me down and calls me names. John's parents were divorced, and he was forced to visit with his dad and stepmom on Wednesdays and every other weekend. As John and I continued our conversations, I realized that he was coming to meet with me almost every Wednesday-- the day he had to visit his father. He would be anxious all day and try to figure out ways not to go to his father's house. As a result, in part, of his dad's treatment of him, John was depressed and starting smoking and drinking. This, of course made things much worse. When I spoke to John's mother about his feelings toward his dad, his mother knew how John felt, but felt helpless to change the situation. John continued with the counseling but continued to have difficulties. Now that John has graduated from high school, he rarely sees his father.

The next type of parenting style is the **Permissive Parent**. The permissive parent is more relaxed and want to establish more of a friendship type of relationship with their children. Discipline is rare and the children are left to do pretty much whatever they want. I have heard parents say that their parents were authoritarian, and they did not want to raise their children that way. Unfortunately, these parents have gone to the extreme opposite parenting style. According to Madeline Levine, in permissive households,
"rules are enforced erratically and children in these household have few responsibilities. The children of permissive parents have little sense that the adults in the house are the ones who are in charge."[2]

The students I have worked with who were from permissive homes were friendly and outgoing but also didn't really understand boundaries and limitations as it related to their actions. Sometimes when these kids had difficulty at school, they were surprised by the consequences received or the negative reactions to their behavior. A few years ago, I co-facilitated a program called "Insight." This was created for students who violated the drug and alcohol policies of the school district. The students that were referred to the program had to attend three 2-hour sessions with one or both of their parents. In exchange, the suspension time was reduced for students who attended these sessions. The program included students sharing with the group what brought them there, exercises that the parents and students did together along with informational videos and discussions. In one session, a father was quite annoyed that he had to attend these sessions with his daughter, who was turned in for smoking marijuana at a school event. This father complained that pot was legal in some states, and he didn't see any problem with his daughter's pot use. This father was permissive, and his daughter suffered as a result.

The Authoritative Parent is another parenting style that is talked about frequently. "Authoritative parents are responsive to the child's emotional need while having high standards. They set limits and are very consistent in enforcing boundaries. (Google. Jan. 15, 2021). According to Levine, "…support, rather than criticism or punishment, is typically used to encourage children to meet expectations. Authoritative parents promote autonomy by encouraging their own children to figure out how to approach challenges on their own, rather than prematurely stepping in and problem-solving for them."[3]

The students I have encountered who had authoritative parents were self-confident in their abilities and were willing to try new things and solve problems. When and if these kids got in trouble, they were devastated about disappointing their parents, but not in a fearful way. They genuinely did not want to disappoint their parents. The high regard and mutual respect are very clear with this type of parenting.

As I have interacted with parents over the years, I came up with my own names for the variety of parents that I have encountered. Three distinct styles stood out. I like to call these styles Blackhawk Betty, Hands Off Harry, and Consistent Carrie. Another style that also stands out is Blaming Bob. There were many occasions I encountered parents who had unpleasant middle school and high school experiences. Their feelings about those experiences resurfaced as their child entered those grades. Those conversations and meetings went something like this: "I'm hopeful that Johnny can have a good middle school experience. I didn't do so well in school, and I want him to have a better experience than I did." I could visibly see and hear the anxiety in these parents' voices and faces. They were scared to death to have their children enter middle school. Many parents are very involved at the elementary level and are in uncharted waters with how to interact with their children in middle school. Some parents are still hovering and wanting to "oversee" their child's every move. Other parents feel the need to back away as their child enters middle school. Two distinct styles stood out. I like to call these styles Blackhawk Betty and Hands-off Harry.

The Black Hawk Betty parents (similar to Authoritarian) used to be referred to as "helicopter" parents. The Blackhawk helicopter is used for a variety of military missions and is much bigger than a traditional helicopter. As it relates in this scenario regarding parenting types, the Blackhawk parent is more involved and more "hovering" over their children. I understand that parents worry and want to keep their kids safe, but sometimes it's more than is necessary. I am reminded of a parent who called me wanting to know why her son was marked absent from his history class. Parents can log on to our school attendance system and check student attendance. This is something that parents can do at the end of the day or at the end of the week. I was quite surprised that this parent had time during the day to check her son's attendance. I had not intended on calling this parent to tell her why her son came to visit me, but since she called me right after he left my office, I felt compelled to tell her the reason for her son's visit to my office. The Blackhawk parents want to know what is going on with their children every second of the day. If a grade seems amiss, they are emailing the teacher immediately instead of letting the child investigate on their own, taking them back to the enabling behaviors. These parents often make excuses for their child's behaviors and want to fix every situation. These parents also criticize their children, especially as it relates to their child's schoolwork or lack thereof.

The other type of parenting style I encountered over the years was the parent I like to call Hands-off Harry. This type of parent is similar to Permissive. They tend to send their child to school and expects the school to do the work. These parents don't come to school for any reason. They often sign up for parent-teacher conferences, but then don't show up. They rarely respond to emails that the teachers send giving updates about their child's performance. This type of parent never surfaces until the end of the grading period and then wants to know why their child is failing. They often storm into the school, wanting to confront teachers and administrators as to why we didn't help their child. I have had many conversations with this type of parent. I ask them if they have checked their child's grades online or reached out to teachers. The responses I get in return are varied. Some parents lament that they are working all the time and have not looked at grades. Other parents say that they are not computer savvy and don't know how to access the online grading system. The child of this type of parent is embarrassed when their parent does "show up" asking questions. They are used to just handling things on their own.

The Blaming Bobs are like the Hands-off Harry. They simply want to blame the school. This type of parent wants the school to do the parenting. Those parents feel that we should somehow "fix" their child. These parents have little interest in being part of the process and working collaboratively with the school. I realize that this type of parent is struggling with issues that teachers and administers are not aware of. This type of parent may be too embarrassed to ask for help or doesn't know where to begin to work with the school. A few years ago, I made a phone call to a parent early one morning. I wanted to let her know that her son was not doing his work in several classes and had gotten into some minor trouble at school. This mother immediately became defensive and told me she was tired of dealing with her son's behavior. She then told me that she didn't have time to deal with this and hung up. I'm not judging these parents, just simply pointing out some of the parenting styles I have encountered. I realize that parents have their hands full juggling work, home, and teenaged children. We are in this education thing together and the more collaboration we have with parents, the better the child will be. It still takes a village.

The final parenting style I have witnessed, I like to call Consistent Carrie. The Consistent Carrie's support their children like the Authoritative parents, but they don't hover, and they only get involved when they have to. The children of Consistent Carrie's, have confidence to handle most of their issues but are not afraid to ask for help when needed. They have a good relationship with their parents and usually talk to their parents about everything. The Consistent Carrie's don't flip out if some difficulty arises. They are usually well-informed about things happening at school, but also give their children autonomy to manage school and other activities. Teachers love Consistent Carrie's because they know if an issue does arise, it will be dealt with, and the parents will be supportive of the school.

What's Next:

1. Make sure punishment fits the crime.
2. If you are too emotional, take some time to calm down before talking to your child.
3. Be consistent.

Discipline is helping a child solve a problem.
Punishment is making a child suffer for having a problem.
To raise problem solvers, focus on solutions, not retribution.
-L.R. Knost

Kathy Starks

THE ROLE OF ORGANIZED RELIGION

There are no great people in this world, only great challenges which ordinary people rise to meet. ~ William F. Halsey

I recently asked my pastor, Rev. Dr. Jermaine D. Covington what his thoughts were regarding the increased rate of anxiety and depression in children and the increase in teen suicides. His response was swift. His comment was, "It is a lack of fear." I asked what he meant, and he said, "The family has fallen apart because there is no fear. Children don't fear their parents anymore and parents are trying to be friends with their kids. And parents, don't fear God. The order should be God, parent, and child. People are not living a God-fearing life."

Interesting, I thought. For some people in some communities, the role of the church has vanished or is vanishing. Growing up, I was made to go to church; it was non-negotiable. Today many younger parents weren't raised in the church and don't see the need for their children to attend. For me, the church was a place to have friends other than at school, a place to practice public speaking skills and clearly to learn some life lessons.

I recently facilitated a town hall meeting at my church, St. John A.M.E. Church in Columbus, Ohio one Sunday after service. There were about thirty participants. I asked the question: Why do you

64

think there is an increase in teen anxiety and depression? Some people felt that single-parent households were part of the problem. Others felt that kids today spend too much time on social media. Still, others felt that there is a lack of trust between kids and adults. Some individuals believe that there is a stigma around getting help for mental health issues. Parents don't want others to see their child as weak or needing this type of help. My church congregation is predominantly African American, and there is a stigma in some African American families that seeking mental health help is a sign of weakness. Many commented that the church needs to be a part of the village. One member commented that our church leaders need to also be trained in counseling techniques so that if a parent or child comes to them with a concern, they might better be equipped to address the issues and know who else to turn to for help in various situations. The ministers can step out of their ministerial roles at times and just talk to the youth. Parents don't have to be the end all be all for their children. Make sure kids have other adults to talk to.

Another member mentioned that church came first. Now parents schedule sports and other activities on Sundays. Today, many sports teams have games and matches on Sunday mornings, a time that used to be dedicated to the church. The students I know who do attend church enjoy the youth groups and take solace in talking to the youth pastors and other leaders at the church. It's also a way for students to be involved in the community through church-sponsored community-service projects.

The participants in this discussion believe that the church still has a role in family life and is still part of the village. Churches should stand up and take more of a role in children's lives today. Churches need to cater to children and younger families. Churches can provide more opportunities for kids to be involved. Sometime youth pastors are the first to know when a child is struggling. Youth pastors have a way of relating to students that often have a greater impact than a parent, teacher, or counselor. The students I have encountered that are very involved with their church youth group seem to be confident and know that they have support when they need it.

What's Next:

1. Have more youth activities at church.
2. Connect children with youth pastors.
3. Have ministerial staff receive more training in counseling strategies.

HERE'S WHAT THE KIDS HAVE TO SAY

As I began working on this book, I thought it would be a good idea to survey some of the high school students to get their ideas regarding student mental health and other possible issues of concern to teenagers. I surveyed 251 students in grades 9-12. One question was: Do you think more teens today suffer from anxiety and depression? 64.2% of the students responded yes to that question. Of those students, 55% were male students and 68% were female students. It was my thought that more female students would respond yes to that question because I believe social pressures to fit in are greater for girls. When asked some of the causes for the increase in anxiety and depression, 25% of the students cited school related issues as the cause. 14.5% and 13.7% of the students responded that friends and family, respectively were the causes for anxiety and depression. To my surprise, only 7.3% of the students cited social media as a contributing factor for anxiety and depression. When asked what types of things parents should do to ease anxiety and depression, 52.2% of the students said that parents should "listen more." When asked what things teachers should do to ease stress in teens, 46% of the students responded that teachers should "be more lenient with grades."

When the students were asked if they felt that their parents trusted them to make wise decisions regarding friends and their social lives, 60% of the students believe that their parents trust them to make wise decisions.

In the winter of 2021, I had the unique opportunity to work with seven juniors on a research project which continued through the rest of the school year and will continue next year as well. Dr. Keith Bell, from The Ohio State University had a large group of students participate in student research, YPAR (Youth Participatory Action Research). Dr. Bell and his colleagues gathered Central Ohio students to participate in this project. The goal was for each student group was to research an issue in their school population that they wanted to address. Topics ranged from having more participation in extracurricular activities among students to addressing mental health concerns within a school population. The group of students that my colleague and I worked with decided that they wanted to address mental health concerns within our school. We divided the students into two groups. We met via Zoom with Dr. Bell and his team and the other school groups each month from February through May. Each month Dr. Bell had world renowned speakers who joined our meetings to share their thoughts about leadership and share some of the personal obstacles they had faced. Some of our guest presenters included, Clark Kellogg, former NBA basketball player and sports analyst for CBS Sports, Erin Gruwell, educator and author of *The Freedom Writers*, Olympic Gold Medalist, Butch Reynolds, and former NBA basketball star and coach, Jim Clemons. These presenters' stories were so inspiring and uplifting and motivated our students to want to learn from this experience. The students learned how to conduct research and what type of research would be needed for the goals they wanted to accomplish. In May we had the culminating session where all the school groups shared the findings of their research.

What my group discovered was that of the 304 students surveyed, 45% of those students were not aware of the mental health services provided in our building. When the students interviewed the school counselors, the counselors shared that they were seeing an increase in anxiety among their caseload of students this year (20-21), primarily due to COVID-19.

In the research, students also noted that some of the students surveyed were hesitant to come to the counseling office because they didn't want their friends and others to see them there, and they also had some concerns that their counselor would call their parents if they did stop into see them. The students did note, however, that the statistics may be different in the future, post-pandemic, as the school population was in and out of the building this year and it was difficult to build relationships in general. One idea that is being implemented is installing textured film over some of the windows leading into the counseling office so that those passing by cannot see who is waiting to see their counselor.

As the students continue this research, they will explore other ways that counselors and staff can be more engaged with students and assist students in seeking help if they need it during the school day.

Another survey that was recently conducted by the Worthington City Schools was The OHYES Survey (Ohio Healthy Youth Environment Survey) for the 2019-2020 school year. This survey is web-based and is available to schools free of charge and can be conducted every four years.

Superintendents and administrators select the grades and percentage of students who participate. In this survey, 681 Thomas Worthington High School students participated. The survey examines a variety of factors such a sleep habits, participation in sports or extracurricular activities, and mental health issues just to name a few. The survey revealed that 30.75% of the students' exhibited issues with anxiety warranting further exploration by a mental health professional. In addition to that, 22.76% of the students exhibited issues with depression that warranted further exploration from a mental health professional. Many Central Ohio schools are recognizing the need for more school counselors and mental health counselors. The Worthington City schools has already committed to increasing the number of mental health counselors in both high schools for the upcoming school year.

CONCLUSION

During the writing of this book, our world encountered a pandemic on a magnitude that has never been experienced before. Amidst all the devastation across the world, there have been some positives outcomes. One relates to families and time spent together. I have seen and heard parents commenting they have discovered things about their children that they never knew before. Parents are discovering their children's passions and talents. This has been a wonderful outcome of the pandemic. Conversely, there have been some negative outcomes as it relates to families as well. In some households, parents discovered their child's depression and anxiety that they weren't aware of, or they "find" out about educational difficulties that their child was having. I also believe that many children discovered more things about their parents that they didn't know either. Kids got to see their parents at work even though it was via Zoom. I'm sure many kids might not admit it, but they enjoyed having their parents around a bit more.

When you find your passion, you will discover your purpose. The writing of this book has been a passion project for me. I started writing this over 10 years ago when I was facilitating parent workshops. I began putting ideas down on paper and continued to work as a middle school counselor. I forgot about some of the ideas I had already written down.

When I began my work at the high school, a whole new array of opportunities opened as I started to explore and understand the challenges of high school students and the stressors and pressures that they experience. During this time, the book was resurrected, and I began the task of working on the book during the pandemic. The pandemic gave me the opportunity to have Zoom interviews with individuals and talk to a few students as well. I was able to read a few books as references and interview quite a few people also.

I hope you have enjoyed reading this book and gained a bit of understanding of the types of things I have been involved with over the years as a school counselor. It has been six years now since I officially retired, and my friends continue to ask me how long I will work. I can't answer that question at this time. I truly love the staff that I work with and feel like many of the students are my own. I love seeing their growth and development and seeing them persevere through tough times. Being a counselor is not what I do, it's who I am. I believe I was "called" to do this work; to work with children and their families. There is no grater blessing in life than to love and have passion for the work that you do. The more that we can create those opportunities for our children, the happier they will be.

It's not what you do for your children, but what you have taught them to do for themselves that will make them successful human beings. ~ Anne Landers

ACKNOWLEDGMENTS

This work could not have been completed without the help of many of my friends and colleagues who allowed me to interview them, have supported me, and have given me suggestions. I would like to acknowledge and thank the following individuals:

Dr. Nicolya Williams whose "Book Writing Boot Camp" helped me to understand exactly what it takes to write a book and get it published. Her lessons and information were invaluable! Dr. Lakeesha Leonard who consistently kept me on track with deadlines and helped me to understand the "why" of writing this book and bringing it to fruition. Special thanks to my Godson, Camron Hubble for his insight regarding teens today and the stressors they face, and Nia Coleman for sharing her thoughts.

I would also like to thank my coworkers who supported me on this journey; Cindy Stanich, Emma Ruiz, Stephanie Burns, Celeste Preisse, Kelly Swearingen, David Quart, Pete Scully, Liz Keener, Tina Nunez, Bob and Judi Galasso, Stephanie Matson, Kim Thesing, Dr. Dan Girard, and all the Thomas Worthington High School staff and students who completed my surveys. To Jummy Olawale and Joan Zeller, therapists whose knowledge and insight are so very much appreciated. To Lori Povisil, my partner in all the parent workshops we facilitated, thanks for friendship and collaboration. A special thanks to Felicha Smith and her son Jaden, and to my former student Eli Malench, who were courageous enough to share their stories with me.

To my mentor and friend Antoinette Miranda, and to Kay Warren, educator and friend, for reading my book early on and giving me so much encouragement and ideas. Your support is greatly appreciated!

To Dr. Keith Bell, Dr. Kirsten Smith, Andrew Smith, Justin Ferguson, Dwight Carter, Joey Gates, Deb Johnson, Carol Taylor, and Dr. Lisa Miller, thank you for allowing me to interview you and hear some of your stories and experiences. I also appreciate the members of St. John African Methodist Episcopal Church, especially Rev. Dr. Jermaine D. Covington, who shared their thoughts and voices during the think tank I facilitated after church one Sunday.

To my brother Kevin and to some of my special friends, who are too many to name, I appreciate your words of wisdom and support through this entire journey. I couldn't have done this without you! To Wilma Burton of 3 Sisters Design, thank you for the cover design work and your patience through all the various drafts. I appreciate you! To my publishing and editing team of Erica Anderson, Kayla Brissi and Dr. Nicolya Williams, this book could not have been completed without your support and guidance. I am beyond grateful to you!

REFERENCES

Kahlil Gibran, *The Prophet,* (New York: Alfred A. Knopf, Inc., 1923)

The Village

1. Ron Taffel, *The Second Family,* (New York: St. Martin's Press, 2001)

Chapter 1 – Enabling Behaviors

1. Jessica Lahey, *The Gift of Failure,* (New York: Harper, 2015) XXI, pg., 47, 136.

2. Julie Lythcott-Haims, *How To Raise An Adult,* (New York: St. Martin's Griffin, 2015) Pg. 74

3. Insider.com, May 25, 2021

4. Madeline Levine, *The Price of Privilege,* (New York: Harper, 2006) pg. 14

5. Jessica Lahey, *The Gift of Failure,* (New York: Harper, 2015) pg. 77

Chapter 2 – Middle School and The Teenage Brain

1. David Walsh, *Why Do They Act That Way?* (New York: Free Press, 2004) Pg. 60

2. Jessica Lahey, *The Gift of Failure,* (New York: Harper, 2015) pg. 136

3. David Walsh, *Why Do They Act That Way?* (New York: Free Press, 2004) Pg. 145

Chapter 3 – The Role of Sleep

1.   James Gangwisch, *How Sleeping Late Can Lead to Depression.* (Todd Neal, Medpage Today, January 1, 2010)

Chapter 4 – The Role of Sports

1.   My Story – Felicha Smith and Jaden Smith, May 5, 2021

Chapter 5 – Helping Children Create Their Legacies: Finding Purpose and Passion

1.   John C. Maxwell, *The 15 Laws of Invaluable Growth,* (New York: Center Street, 2012) pg. 162

Chapter 6 – The Family as a System

1.   Betterhelp.com, August 11, 2021. Family Systems Therapy

2.   Jessica Lahey, *The Gift of Failure,* (New York: Harper, 2015) pg. 47

Chapter 7 – Exposure and experience can expand Potential

1.   Elijah Malench, "My Career Path" April 21, 2021.

2.   Thomas Armstrong, Ph.D. Multiple Intelligences. www.institute4learning.com. (M.I Image)

3.   Mslilyteacher.com. Multiple Intelligence: Why Not Measure Our Children's Strengths? (2017) (M.I Image)

Chapter 8 – Resilience

1.	Madeline Levine, *The Price of Privilege,* (New York: Harper, 2006) pg. 77

Chapter 9 - Parenting Styles and Discipline

1.	Madeline Levine, *The Price of Privilege,* (New York: Harper, 2006) pg. 106

2.	Madeline Levine, *The Price of Privilege,* (New York: Harper, 2006) pg. 130

3.	Madeline Levine, *The Price of Privilege,* (New York: Harper, 2006) pg. 131

Interviews with the author

1. Camron Hubble, October 10, 2021

2. Jummy Olawale, May 23, 2021

3. Keith Bell, Ph.D., April 25, 2021

4. Jeffrey Maddox, September 13, 2021

5. Kirsten Smith, Ph.D. and Andrew Smith, April 2, 2021

6. Pete Scully, February 18, 2021

7. Deb Johnson, June 6, 2021

8. Lisa Miller, Ph.D., May 7, 2021

9. Joan Zeller, March 2021

10. Carol Taylor, February 2021

11. Rev. Dr. Jermaine D. Covington, February 2020

Kathy Starks was born and raised in Columbus, Ohio and has had a passion for helping teens most of her adult life. Initially trained as a speech therapist at Bowling Green State University, Starks worked in a state high school which was part of the juvenile corrections system for eight years. Starks realized that she was more interested in the "why" of what caused the teens to get in trouble, instead of caring about their speech and hearing difficulties. This led her to earn a master's in counseling, at The Ohio State University which has been her focus over the last twenty-five plus years.

Kathy was also a student who struggled academically in middle and high school, and she understands those students who struggle and feels a connection with those who find middle and high school challenging. Because of this connection, she likes to call herself the "Kid Whisperer."

Starks has had the opportunity to facilitate a variety of parent workshops on the topic of understanding the middle school child as well as career development.

Kathy's other passion is tennis, and she enjoys coaching and playing with the students at her high school.

You can find Kathy on the following platforms:

www.facebook.com/authorkathystarks

www.linkedin.com/in/kathy-starks-author

www.ingramcontent.com/pod-product-compliance
Lightning Source LLC
Chambersburg PA
CBHW062023040426
42447CB00010B/2111